Jams, Jellies & Preserves

CHARTWELL
BOOKS, INC.

Published by Chartwell Books
a division of Book Sales, Inc.
114 Northfield Avenue
Edison, NJ 08837

This edition produced for sale
in the U.S.A., its territories
and dependencies only.

ISBN 0-7858-0424-2

Conceived, designed and produced by Haldane Mason, London

Printed in Italy

Note: Cup measurements in this book are for standard American cups. Unless otherwise stated, milk is assumed to be full-fat. All butter is sweet unless otherwise stated.

CONTENTS

CLASSIC STRAWBERRY CONSERVE

MAKES 6 x 1 lb JARS

3 quarts fresh strawberries, hulled

8 cups granulated sugar

Whole fruit is used to make a conserve, and the finished consistency is thinner and more syrupy than jam. This homemade conserve is a real treat – make some to spoon onto warm, fresh biscuits.

1 Place alternate layers of strawberries and sugar in a very large bowl (or use two smaller bowls). Cover and leave in a cool place for 24 hours.

2 Transfer the strawberry mixture to a large, heavy-based pan. Heat gently, stirring occasionally, until boiling. Boil steadily for 5 minutes.

3 Remove the pan from the heat, then return the mixture to the bowl. Cover with a clean, damp dish towel and leave in a cool place for 2 days.

4 Transfer the mixture to the pan once more. Bring to the boil, then boil steadily for 10–20 minutes, until a soft set is reached. To test for a soft set, place a teaspoonful of the conserve on a cold saucer and cool it quickly. Push the surface with your finger – it should crinkle slightly if at all, but should not be stiff.

5 Sterilize the jars by washing them in hot, soapy water. Rinse in hot water, then place them in a preheated oven at 250°F until they are needed for filling.

4

6 Leave the conserve to stand for 15–20 minutes, then stir to distribute the fruit. Pour into the warmed, sterilized jars, seal and label.

BLACKCURRANT JAM

Blackcurrants are one of the finest fruits for jam making. They have a delicious sharp-sweet flavor, and a high pectin content, which helps the jam to set.

MAKES 6 x 1 lb JARS

2 quarts blackcurrants

3½ cups water

6 cups granulated sugar

1 Check over the fruit to remove any stalks and leaves, but avoid washing the fruit unless really necessary. Put into a preserving pan or other very large pan with the water. Heat and simmer gently for 30–40 minutes to soften the fruit and release the pectin, which helps the jam to set.

2 Add the sugar to the blackcurrants and let it dissolve, stirring occasionally. Bring to the boil and boil rapidly until setting point is reached – about 15–20 minutes. Skim off any scum, not foam, toward the end of cooking time. To test for setting point, spoon a little jam onto a cold saucer and cool it quickly. Push the jam with your finger – it should crinkle on the surface, but should not be stiff. Double check by putting a drop of cooled jam on the end of your finger. If the jam does not run off, it is ready.

3 When the jam has reached setting point

remove it from the heat and allow it to settle for a few minutes. Stir, then pour into warmed, sterilized jars (see page 4). Seal and label. The jam will set as it cools.

GOOSEBERRY JAM

This is a true country-style jam, which creates delightful memories of hot, hazy midsummer days when you eat it in the middle of winter.

MAKES 10 x 1 lb JARS

scant 3 quarts gooseberries, not too ripe

3 cups water

10–12 heads of elderflowers (optional)

3–4 sprigs of tansy (optional)

10 cups granulated sugar

1 Trim the ends of the gooseberries. Place them in a preserving pan or other very large pan and add the water. Carefully rinse the elderflower heads and tansy (if using), then tie them in a cheesecloth bag. Add to the pan. Heat and simmer gently, stirring occasionally, until the fruit is soft and tender – about 20–30 minutes.

2 Meanwhile, place the sugar in a large heatproof bowl. Transfer to a preheated oven at 300°F for 15–20 minutes to warm through.

3 Remove the pan from the heat and lift out the cheesecloth bag, squeezing out any juice from the bag back into the pan. Discard the bag. Add the warmed sugar to the pan and leave it to dissolve, stirring gently from time to time.

4 Return the pan to the heat and bring to the boil. Boil steadily until setting point is reached. To test for setting point, spoon a little jam onto a cold saucer and cool it quickly. Push the surface of the jam with your finger – it should crinkle, but should not be stiff.

5 Remove the pan from the heat and let the jam settle for a few minutes. Stir to distribute the fruit evenly, then pour into warmed, sterilized jars (see page 4). Seal and label.

RASPBERRY & REDCURRANT JAM

Ripe summer fruits combine perfectly to give a clear, bright jam that makes a beautiful spread for fresh bread, toast and muffins

MAKES 10 x 1 lb JARS

3 quarts raspberries

2 quarts redcurrants

1¼ cups water

12 cups granulated sugar

1 Pick over the raspberries and redcurrants, discarding any stalks. Put them into a very large pan or preserving pan with the water. Heat gently and simmer until the fruit is softened, about 20–25 minutes. Remove the preserving pan from the heat.

2 Add the sugar to the fruit and stir until dissolved. Return the pan to the heat and bring the mixture to the boil. Boil rapidly until setting point is reached. To test for setting point, spoon a little jam onto a cold saucer and cool it quickly. Push the surface of the jam with your finger – it should crinkle, but should not be stiff.

3 Remove the pan from the heat and leave the jam to settle for a few minutes. Stir to distribute the fruit evenly, then pour into warmed, sterilized jars (see page 4). Seal and label.

SUMMER PUDDING JAM

MAKES 6 x 1 lb JARS

2 quarts blackcurrants

1½ pints strawberries, hulled

2 cups redcurrants

2 cups raspberries

1½ quarts water

12 cups granulated sugar

Make the most of the wonderful variety of soft summer fruit by preserving some in this superb jam. Strawberries, raspberries, blackcurrants, and redcurrants are perfect because they taste so good together!

1 Remove any stalks and leaves from the fruit, but avoid washing it unless really necessary. Put it into a preserving pan or other very large pan with the water. Heat and simmer gently for 30–40 minutes. This softens the fruit and releases the pectin, which helps the jam to set.

2 Remove pan from the heat. Add the sugar to the fruit and leave to dissolve completely, stirring the mixture from time to time. Bring to the boil and boil rapidly until setting point is reached – about 15–20 minutes. Skim off any scum toward the end of cooking time. To test for setting point, spoon a little jam onto a cold saucer and cool it quickly. Push the jam with your finger – it should crinkle on the surface, but should not be stiff.

3 Pour the jam into warmed, sterilized jars (see page 4), then seal and label. The jam will set as it cools.

12

BLACKBERRY & APPLE JAM

Blackberries growing wild are combined with windfall apples to make this into a very economical, yet extremely delicious recipe for jam.

MAKES 10 x 1 lb JARS

4 lb blackberries

1¼ cups water

2 lb apples

12 cups granulated sugar

1 Pick over the blackberries, discarding any stalks. Put them into a very large pan or preserving pan with half the water. Heat gently and simmer until the fruit is softened, about 20–25 minutes.

2 Meanwhile, peel, core, and chop the apples and cook them in a separate pan with the remaining water, until they are soft. Add the apples to the blackberries, stir together, then remove the pan from the heat.

3 Add the sugar to the fruit and stir until dissolved. Return the pan to the heat and bring the mixture to the boil. Boil rapidly until setting point is reached. To test for setting point, spoon a little jam onto a cold saucer and cool it quickly. Push the surface of the jam with your finger – it should crinkle, but should not be stiff.

4 Remove the pan from the heat and leave the jam to settle for a few minutes. Stir to

distribute the fruit evenly, then
pour into warmed, sterilized jars
(see page 4). Seal and label.

15

FALL FRUIT JAM

3 lb apples
2 lb pears
1¼ cups water
2 lb plums
12 cups granulated sugar

In this jam, a combination of fall fruits is used to make a preserve with an excellent flavor. Choose apples, pears, and plums that are not over-ripe for the best flavor and consistency.

1 Peel, core, and chop the apples and pears, and put them into a preserving pan or other very large pan with the water. Halve and pit the plums and add them to the pan.

2 Heat gently and simmer until the fruit is softened, about 20–25 minutes. Remove the pan from the heat.

3 Add the sugar to the fruit and stir until dissolved. Return the pan to the heat and bring to the boil. Boil rapidly until setting point is reached. To test for setting point, spoon a little jam onto a cold saucer and cool it quickly. Push the surface of the jam with your finger – it should crinkle, but should not be stiff.

4 Remove the pan from the heat and leave the jam to settle for a few minutes. Stir to distribute the fruit evenly, then pour into warmed, sterilized jars (see page 4). Seal and label.

MAKES 10 x 1 lb JARS

5 lb rhubarb, trimmed and chopped

1¼ cups water

2 lb crab apples

1½ tbsp lemon juice

12 cups granulated sugar

1 tsp ground cinnamon

2 tsp chopped fresh ginger root (or 1 tsp ground ginger)

RHUBARB & CRAB APPLE JAM

This delightful jam is made with a combination of rhubarb and crab apples. Cinnamon and fresh ginger root lend a lovely, subtle fragrance and flavor.

1 Put the rhubarb into a very large pan or preserving pan with the water. Heat gently and simmer until the fruit is softened, about 10–15 minutes.

2 Meanwhile, peel, core, and chop the crab apples. Add them to pan with the lemon juice, stir together, and cook until softened, about 30 minutes. Remove the pan from the heat.

3 Add the sugar to the fruit and stir until dissolved. Return the pan to the heat and bring the mixture to the boil.

Boil rapidly until setting point is reached. To test for setting point, spoon a little jam onto a cold saucer and cool it quickly. Push the surface of the jam with your finger – it should crinkle, but should not be stiff.

4 Remove the pan from the heat and leave the jam to settle for a few minutes. Stir to distribute the fruit evenly, then add the cinnamon and ginger, stirring well to mix thoroughly.

18

Pour into warmed, sterilized jars
(see page 4), then seal and label.

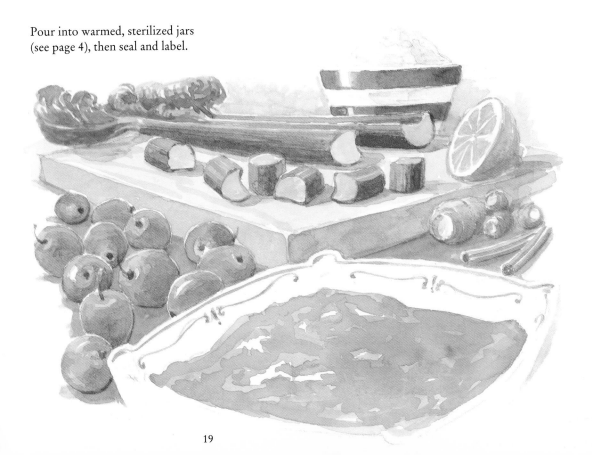

DAMSON PLUM JAM

Sharp-flavored damson plums are small and bluish-purple. They make the most marvelous jam, with a dark, rich color.

MAKES 8 x 1 lb JARS

4 lb damson plums

3 cups water

10 cups granulated sugar

1 Put the damson plums into a very large pan or preserving pan. Do not attempt to remove the pits at this stage as it is much easier to take them out later when the fruit has softened.

2 Add the water and bring to the boil, then reduce the heat and simmer gently until the fruit is soft and the contents of the pan are reduced by one third. Skim off as many of the pits as possible as they are loosened and float to the surface. Remove the pan from the heat.

3 Add the sugar and stir until dissolved. Return to the heat and bring to the boil. Boil rapidly until setting point is reached. To test for setting point, spoon a little jam onto a cold saucer and cool it quickly. Push the surface of the jam with your finger – it should crinkle, but should not be stiff.

4 Remove the pan from the heat and leave the jam to settle for a few minutes. Stir to distribute the fruit evenly, then pour into warmed, sterilized jars (see page 4). Seal and label.

20

GREENGAGE PRESERVE

Greengages are small green plums which have a golden hue when fully ripe. If you enjoy plum jam then this recipe could become one of your favorites.

**MAKES 10 x
1 lb JARS**

6 lb greengages

scant 2 cups water

12 cups granulated sugar

1 Cut the greengages in half and remove their pits. Put the fruit into a very large pan or preserving pan. Remove some of the kernels from the pits and add them to the pan with the water. (The pectin contained in the kernels helps the jam to set.)

2 Heat gently and simmer until the fruit is soft and the contents of the pan are reduced by about one-third. Remove the pan from the heat.

3 Add the sugar and stir until dissolved, then return the pan to the heat. Bring to the boil and boil rapidly until setting point is reached. To test

for setting point, spoon a little jam onto a cold saucer and cool it quickly. Push the surface of the jam with your finger – it should crinkle, but should not be stiff.

4 Remove the pan from the heat and leave the jam to settle for a few minutes. Stir to distribute the fruit evenly, then pour into warmed, sterilized jars (see page 4). Seal and label.

PLUM JAM

Prepare this jam when plums are plentiful. It makes a wonderful topping for baked desserts, and tastes divine with fresh homemade muffins.

MAKES 10 x 1 lb JARS

6 lb medium red plums

scant 2 cups water

12 cups granulated sugar

1 Cut the plums in half and remove their pits. Put the fruit into a preserving pan or other very large pan. Remove some of the kernels from the pits and add them to the pan with the water. (The kernels give the jam a delicious almond flavor and the pectin contained in them helps the jam to set .)

2 Heat gently and simmer until the plums are soft and the contents of the pan are reduced by about a third. Remove the pan from the heat.

3 Add the sugar and stir until dissolved, then return the pan to the heat. Bring to the boil and boil rapidly until setting point is reached. To test for setting point, spoon a little jam onto a cold saucer and cool it quickly. Push the surface of the jam with your finger – it should crinkle, but should not be stiff.

4 Remove the pan from the heat and leave the jam to settle for a few minutes. Skim off as many kernels as possible, then stir to distribute

the fruit evenly. Pour into warmed, sterilized jars (see page 4). Seal and label.

APRICOT & BRANDY CONSERVE

MAKES 7 x 1 lb JARS

2 lb apples

2½ cups water

4 lb fresh apricots, halved and pitted

8 cups granulated sugar

6 tbsp apricot brandy (or use ordinary brandy)

This conserve has a splash of apricot brandy added to give it a bit of a kick. It is lovely to have around at Christmas, when you can have some for breakfast with warm croissants and rolls.

1 Chop the apples roughly, without peeling or coring them. Put them into a large, heavy-based pan with the water and heat gently. Simmer over a low heat, stirring occasionally, until the fruit is very soft – about 1 hour.

2 Strain the fruit through a nylon strainer and retain the strained juice and pulp. (This makes use of the high pectin content of the apples. When the juice and pulp are added to the apricots, the pectin enables the conserve to set.) Discard the pith and seeds.

3 Put the apricots into a large, heavy-based pan or preserving pan with the strained apple juice and pulp. Heat and simmer gently until the fruit is very soft, about 30–40 minutes. Remove from the heat.

4 Add the sugar and stir until dissolved. Return the pan to the heat and bring to the boil. Boil rapidly until a soft set is reached. To test for this, spoon a little conserve onto a cold saucer and cool it quickly. Push the surface with your finger – it should crinkle slightly, but should not be at all stiff.

5 Remove the pan from the heat and leave to settle for a few minutes. Stir in the apricot brandy, then pour the conserve into warmed, sterilized jars (see page 4). Seal and label.

PEACH & HAZELNUT PRESERVE

MAKES 7 x 1 lb JARS

2 lb apples

2½ cups water

4 lb fresh peaches

8 cups granulated sugar

1 cup hazelnuts, halved

Fresh peaches make beautiful jam that tastes very special. This version has a few halved hazelnuts in it, which add an element of luxury to the finished jam.

1 Chop the apples roughly, without peeling or coring them. Put them into a large, heavy-based pan with the water and heat gently. Simmer, stirring occasionally, until the fruit is very soft – about 1 hour.

2 Strain the fruit through a nylon strainer and retain the strained juice and pulp. (This procedure makes use of the high pectin content of the apples. When the juice and pulp are added to the peaches, the pectin helps the jam to set.) Discard the peel, pith and seeds.

3 Cut the peaches into quarters, removing their pits. Put the peaches into a large, heavy-based pan or preserving pan with the apple juice and pulp. Heat and simmer gently for about 20 minutes to soften the peaches, stirring occasionally. Remove the pan from the heat.

4 Add the sugar to the pan and stir until dissolved. Add the hazelnuts, then return the pan to the heat and bring to the boil. Boil rapidly until setting point is reached. To test for setting point, spoon a little jam onto a cold saucer and

cool it quickly. Push the surface of the jam with your finger – it should crinkle, but should not be stiff.

5 Remove the pan from the heat and leave the jam to settle for about 15 minutes. Stir to distribute the fruit and nuts evenly, then pour into warmed, sterilized jars (see page 4). Seal and label.

KUMQUAT & PASSION FRUIT PRESERVE

MAKES 10 x 8 oz JARS

2lb kumquats

4 cups water

⅓ cup lemon juice

4 cups granulated sugar

8 passion fruit

Kumquats look like tiny oval oranges. They have a very thin skin and can be eaten whole, although they are quite sharp. In this delicious recipe they are married with the flavor of passion fruit to create an exotic jam.

1 Slice the kumquats in half. Put them into a large, heavy-based pan with the water. Heat and simmer gently for about 1 hour, until the fruit is very soft. Remove the pan from the heat.

2 Add the lemon juice and sugar to the pan and stir until the sugar has dissolved. Return the pan to the heat and bring the mixture to the boil. Boil rapidly until setting point is reached. To test for setting point, spoon a little jam onto a cold saucer and cool it quickly. Push the surface of the jam with your finger – it should crinkle, but should not be stiff.

3 Remove the pan from the heat and leave the jam to settle for a few minutes. Add the pulp and seeds from the passion fruit and stir to distribute the fruit evenly. Pour into small, warmed, sterilized jars (see page 4). Seal and label.

PEAR & GINGER JAM

Preserved ginger in syrup gives a delicious flavor to this unusual pear jam. Choose firm pears in preference to ones that are very ripe.

1 Peel and core the pears and apples, retaining both the peel and the cores. Tie the peel and cores in a cheesecloth bag. Chop the fruit roughly.

2 Put the fruit into a very large pan or preserving pan with the lemon rind and juice. Add the water and the cheesecloth bag. Bring to the boil, then reduce the heat and simmer gently until the fruit is tender.

3 Remove the pan from the heat and lift out the cheesecloth bag, squeezing any juice from it back into the pan. Discard the bag. Add the sugar to the pan and stir gently until dissolved.

4 Return the pan to the heat and bring to the boil. Boil rapidly until setting point is reached. To test for setting point, spoon a little jam onto a cold saucer and cool it quickly. Push the jam with your finger – it should crinkle on the surface, but should not be stiff.

5 Leave the jam to settle for 15 minutes, then add the ginger. Stir to distribute the fruit and ginger. Pour into warmed,

sterilized jars (see page 4), then
seal and label.

FIG & WALNUT CONSERVE

MAKES 4 x 1 lb JARS

2 lb fresh figs, quartered

finely grated rind of 2 lemons

⅓ cup lemon juice

4 tbsp water

4 cups granulated sugar

½ cup walnut halves

This delightful Fig & Walnut Conserve tastes excellent with toast or fresh rolls at breakfast time. Try a little spooned onto creamy rice pudding or semolina to make a delicious dessert.

1 Put the figs into a large heavy-based pan with the lemon rind and juice. Add the water and cook over a gentle heat, stirring occasionally, until the figs are soft.

2 Meanwhile, place the sugar in a large heatproof bowl. Place in a preheated oven at 300°F for 15–20 minutes to warm through.

3 Tip the warmed sugar into the figs and stir gently to avoid breaking up the fruit. Heat until the sugar has dissolved, then bring to the boil. Boil the mixture steadily until a soft set is reached. To test for a soft set, place a teaspoonful of the conserve onto a cold saucer and cool it quickly. Push the surface with your finger – it should crinkle slightly, but should not be at all stiff.

4 Leave the conserve for 10–15 minutes to let it settle, then add the walnuts. Stir gently to distribute the fruit and nuts, then pour into warmed, sterilized jars (see page 4). Seal and label.

PINEAPPLE JAM

**MAKES 3 x
1 lb JARS**

**8 cups canned crushed pineapple
in natural juice**

4 tbsp lemon juice

8 cups granulated sugar

This jam uses canned crushed pineapple for speed, convenience, and economy. It has a great flavor and tastes good in sandwiches, especially with some sliced banana. You can also use this jam for cake fillings or for spreading on toast.

1 Put the pineapple and lemon juice into a large, heavy-based pan. Heat and simmer gently, uncovered, until thickened and pulpy. Remove the pan from the heat.

2 Add the sugar and stir until dissolved. Return the pan to the heat and bring to the boil. Boil rapidly until setting point is reached. To test for setting point, spoon a little jam onto a cold saucer and cool it quickly. Push the surface of the jam with your finger – it should crinkle, but should not be stiff.

3 Leave the jam to settle for a few minutes, then stir. Pour into warmed, sterilized jars (see page 4). Seal and label.

ORANGE MARMALADE

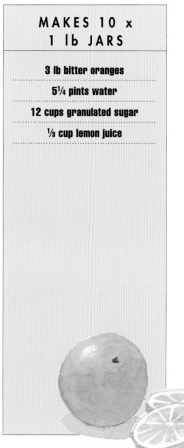

MAKES 10 x 1 lb JARS

3 lb bitter oranges

5¼ pints water

12 cups granulated sugar

⅓ cup lemon juice

At the end of the winter, fill the house with the wonderful, bitter-sweet aroma of oranges as they cook to make this most delicious marmalade.

1 Cut the oranges in half and squeeze the juice. Place the seeds in a cheesecloth bag and tie securely. Shred the peel thinly, without removing the pith. Put the peel, juice, cheesecloth bag, and water into a very large pan or preserving pan.

2 Heat and simmer gently for about 2 hours, until the peel is very tender and the contents of the pan are reduced by about one third. Remove the pan from the heat.

3 Lift the cheesecloth bag from the pan and squeeze it to extract the juice, then discard the bag. Add the sugar and lemon juice to the pan and stir constantly until the sugar has dissolved, then return the pan to the heat. Bring to the boil, then boil rapidly until setting point is reached. To test for setting point, spoon a little marmalade onto a cold saucer and cool it quickly. Push the surface of the marmalade with your finger – it should crinkle, but should not be stiff.

4 Skim off any scum from the surface of the marmalade, then remove the pan from the heat. Leave the marmalade to settle for about 15 minutes, then

stir to distribute the shreds evenly. Pour into warmed, sterilized jars (see page 4). Seal and label.

SHARP CITRUS MARMALADE

MAKES 10 x 1 lb JARS

2 lb grapefruit

1 lb sweet oranges

4 limes

6½ pints water

12 cups granulated sugar

Grapefruit, oranges, and limes make this sharp, tangy marmalade. Shred the peel very finely to make it look attractive in the finished preserve.

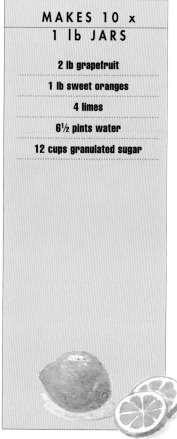

1 Peel the grapefruit and oranges and cut the pith away from the peel. Halve the limes and squeeze the juice. Finely shred the peel from all the fruit and put into a large pan or preserving pan with the lime juice and half the water. Heat and simmer gently until the peel is very tender, about 2 hours.

2 Chop the flesh and pith from both the grapefruit and oranges and place in a large pan with the remaining water. Heat and simmer gently, covered, for about 1¼ hours. Strain through a nylon strainer, then add the strained mixture to the shreds in the other pan (after they have cooked for 2 hours). Remove the pan from the heat.

3 Add the sugar to the pan and stir until dissolved. Return the pan to the heat and bring to the boil. Boil rapidly until setting point is reached. To test for setting point, spoon a little marmalade onto a cold saucer and cool it quickly. Push the surface of the marmalade with your finger – it should crinkle, but should not be stiff.

4 Skim off any scum from the surface, remove the pan from the heat. Leave the marmalade to settle for about 15 minutes, then stir to distribute the shreds evenly. Pour into warmed, sterilized jars (see page 4). Seal and label.

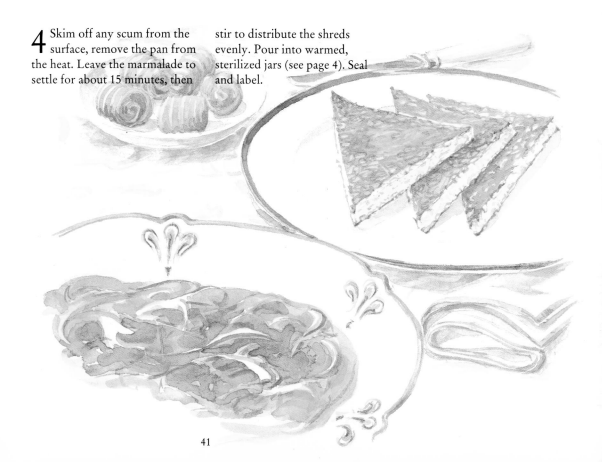

WHISKEY MAC MARMALADE

**MAKES 10 x
1 lb JARS**

3 lb bitter oranges

2½ quarts water

12 cups granulated sugar

4 tbsp lemon juice

**½ cup preserved ginger in
syrup, drained and chopped**

¼ cup ginger wine

½ cup whiskey

*This is strictly a marmalade for the adults, with its
sophisticated flavors of bitter oranges, preserved ginger,
whiskey, and ginger wine.*

1 Cut the oranges in half and squeeze the juice. Place the seeds in a cheesecloth bag and tie securely. Shred the peel thinly, without removing the pith. Put the peel, juice, bag, and water into a very large pan or preserving pan.

2 Bring to the boil and then simmer gently for about 2 hours, until the peel is very tender and the contents of the pan are reduced by about one-third. Remove the pan from the heat.

3 Lift the cheesecloth bag from the pan and squeeze it to extract the juice, then discard the bag. Add the sugar and lemon juice to the pan and stir until the sugar has dissolved, then return the pan to the heat. Bring to the boil, then boil rapidly until setting point is reached. To test for setting point, spoon a little marmalade onto a cold saucer and cool it quickly. Push the surface of the marmalade with your finger – it should crinkle, but should not be stiff.

4 Skim off any scum from the surface of the marmalade, then remove the pan from the heat. Leave the marmalade to settle for about 15 minutes, then add the ginger, ginger wine, and whiskey, stirring well. Pour into warmed, sterilized jars (see page 4). Seal and label.

42

ORANGE & GRAPEFRUIT SPREAD

Fresh homemade Orange and Grapefruit Spread is a real treat, especially when spread generously on crusty new bread or toast for breakfast, or used as a delicious filling for layer cakes.

1 In a large heatproof mixing bowl whisk together the eggs, sugar, orange rind and juice, and grapefruit juice. Add the warm melted butter and stir together.

2 Set the bowl over a large pan of gently simmering water and stir the mixture with a wooden spoon until it thickens, about 10–15 minutes. Check that it is thick enough by lifting the wooden spoon a little and drizzling the mixture over the surface – it should be thick enough to leave a trail. The spread will thicken more as it cools.

3 Pour into warmed, sterilized jars (see page 4). Seal and label. When completely cool, store in the refrigerator. Use within 4–6 weeks. Once opened, eat within a few days.

44

LEMON & LIME SPREAD

With its simple ingredients of butter, sugar, eggs, and citrus fruit, you couldn't wish for a more delicious spread for fresh bread. This recipe is very similar to lemon spread, and includes limes to give a slightly sharper flavor.

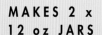

MAKES 2 x 12 oz JARS

4 eggs

1 cup superfine sugar

finely grated rind of 2 large lemons

⅓ cup lemon juice

finely grated rind of 2 limes

¼ cup lime juice

1 cup butter, melted

1 Beat the eggs in a large heatproof bowl. Add the superfine sugar, lemon rind and juice, and lime rind and juice. Cut the butter into pieces and add to the bowl.

2 Set the bowl over a pan of gently simmering water and stir with a wooden spoon until the butter melts and the mixture thickens, about 15–20 minutes. Check that it is thick enough by lifting the wooden spoon a little and drizzling the mixture over the surface – it should be thick enough to leave a trail. The lemon and lime spread will thicken more as it cools.

3 Pour into warmed, sterilized jars (see page 4). Seal and label. When completely cool, store in the refrigerator. Use within 4–6 weeks. Once opened, eat within a few days.

46

BANANA & NECTARINE SPREAD

MAKES 2 x 1 lb JARS

3 large bananas, peeled and chopped

3 nectarines or peaches, peeled, pitted, and chopped

finely grated rind of 1 lemon

4 tbsp lemon juice

½ cup butter

1 cup superfine sugar

4 eggs

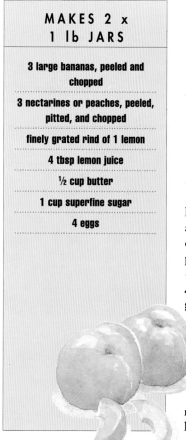

Bananas and nectarines give a new slant to an old favorite. If you love lemon spread, then you will enjoy this scrumptious alternative. Children will like this spread on slices of fresh bread.

1 Put the bananas and nectarines or peaches into a large pan with the lemon rind and juice. Heat gently, stirring often, until the fruit is soft and pulpy – about 5 minutes.

2 Add the butter and sugar to the pan and heat gently, stirring, to melt the butter and dissolve the sugar. Transfer the mixture to a large heatproof bowl and leave to cool for 10 minutes.

3 Beat the eggs and stir them into the fruit mixture. Set the bowl over a large pan of gently simmering water and cook, stirring with a wooden spoon, until the mixture thickens – about 15–20 minutes. To check that it is thick enough, lift the wooden spoon a little and drizzle the mixture over the surface – it should be thick enough to leave a trail. The banana and nectarine spread will thicken more as it cools.

4 Pour into warmed, sterilized jars (see page 4). Seal and label. When completely cool, store in the refrigerator. Use within 4–6 weeks. Once opened, eat within a few days.

APPLE BUTTER

With its soft consistency, Apple Butter makes a delicious spread for fresh bread and rolls. Once a jar is opened store it in the refrigerator and use within 4 weeks.

MAKES 2 x 1 lb JARS

3 lb apples

2½ cups unsweetened apple juice

4 cups granulated sugar

1 tsp ground apple pie spice (optional)

1 Chop the apples roughly, without peeling or coring them. Put them into a large pan together with the apple juice. Bring to the boil, and then simmer gently, uncovered, until the apples are very soft and pulpy, stirring from time to time. Remove the pan from the heat.

2 Rub the apple pulp through a nylon strainer, to remove the peel and seeds. Discard what is left in the strainer and measure the apple pulp. For every 2 cups of apple pulp, measure out 1½ cups sugar.

3 Return the apple pulp to the pan. Heat and simmer until thick, stirring frequently. Add the sugar and stir until dissolved. Cook gently for 25–35 minutes until there is no liquid left in the pan and a wooden spoon drawn through the middle of the mixture leaves a clear trail. Stir in the apple pie spice, if using.

4 Pour into warmed, sterilized jars (see page 4). Top with a wax disc and seal at once. Label and use within 4 weeks. Once opened, eat within a few days.

SPICED MANGO BUTTER

Treat yourself to some of this smooth Spiced Mango Butter. It tastes superb as an exotic topping for pancakes and waffles with a drizzle of maple syrup, or just try it spread generously on crusty new bread.

MAKES 2 x 1 lb JARS

6 large mangoes

1¼ cups unsweetened apple juice

2 cinnamon sticks

6 cloves

½ tsp freshly ground nutmeg

4 cups granulated sugar

1 Slice the mangoes on each side of their large, flat pits. Chop the flesh roughly, without peeling. Put the fruit into a large pan with their pits and the apple juice. Bring to the boil and simmer gently, uncovered, until the mangoes are very soft and pulpy, stirring from time to time. Remove the pan from the heat.

2 Remove the pits from the pan and discard them. Rub the mango pulp through a nylon strainer, to remove the peel. Discard the contents of the strainer, and measure the pulp.

For every 2 cups mango pulp, measure out 1½ cups sugar.

3 Return the mango pulp to the pan. Add the cinnamon sticks, cloves, and nutmeg. Heat and simmer until thick, stirring often. Add the sugar and stir until dissolved. Cook gently until there is no liquid left in the pan and a wooden spoon drawn through the middle of the mixture leaves a clear trail.

4 Remove the cinnamon sticks from the mixture, then pour the mango butter into warmed,

sterilized jars (see page 4). Top
with a wax disc and seal at once.
Label when cool. After opening,
store in the refrigerator and use
within 3 weeks.

PLUMS IN WINE SYRUP

Choose three different varieties of plum to enhance the appearance of this delicious preserve.

MAKES 4 x 2 lb JARS

2 lb medium red plums

2 lb greengages

2 lb medium yellow plums

4 cups water

3 cups granulated sugar

4 cups medium red wine

10 cloves

1 tsp ground allspice

1 Halve the plums and remove their pits. Pack an equal quantity of each type of plum tightly into sterilized preserving jars.

2 Put the water and sugar into a large pan and heat gently, stirring occasionally, until the sugar has dissolved. Bring to the boil and boil for 1 minute. Add the wine and spices, bring back to the boil, then remove from the heat.

3 Pour the wine syrup into the jars to cover the fruit, leaving ½ inch space at the top. Tap the jars lightly to let any air bubbles escape. Put the rubber rings and tops on the jars, but not the clips or screw bands.

4 Stand the jars on a baking tray, leaving plenty of room around each jar for air to circulate. Place in a preheated oven at 300°F for 50 minutes. Remove the jars from the oven one at a time, putting on the clips or tightening the screw bands at once.

5 To check that a vacuum has been made, leave the jars to stand undisturbed for 24 hours, then remove the clip tops or screw bands. Using the fingers of one hand, pick up the jars by the lid – if the lid comes away, a vacuum has not been created. If this happens, the fruit must be eaten straightaway, or be processed for a second time.

TRADITIONAL MINCEMEAT

This excellent homemade mincemeat really packs a punch with its rum-soaked fruit! Try some in your mince pies to give them a wonderful flavor.

MAKES 4 x 1 lb JARS

½ cup candied cherries

⅓ cup candied peel

3 cups raisins

2 cups golden raisins

1⅓ cups white raisins

⅔ cup dark rum, brandy, or sherry

2 medium apples

2 tsp apple pie spice

½ tsp freshly grated nutmeg

1 cup chopped almonds

1⅓ cups molasses sugar, dark muscovado sugar, or dark brown sugar

1½ cups shredded suet or vegetarian suet

1 Halve the candied cherries and chop the candied peel.

2 Put the raisins, golden raisins, white raisins, cherries, candied peel, and rum, brandy, or sherry into a large bowl, mixing well. Cover and leave in a cool, dark place, stirring occasionally, for 1–2 days.

3 Peel, core, and finely chop the apples. Blanch in boiling water for 2 minutes, and then drain well. Add to the soaked dried fruit mixture with the apple pie spice, nutmeg, and chopped almonds, stirring well.

4 Add the molasses sugar, dark muscovado sugar, or dark brown sugar to the fruit mixture and stir well to combine thoroughly. Mix in the shredded suet.

5 Pack into sterilized jars (see page 4), seal and label.

APPLE & MINT JELLY

Perfect with roast lamb and new potatoes, this jelly also tastes very pleasant with fish and chicken dishes.

**MAKES 5 x
1 lb JARS**

6 lb apples

½ cup lemon juice

water

granulated sugar

2 tbsp chopped fresh mint

1 Chop the apples roughly, without peeling or coring them. Put them into a very large pan or preserving pan and add the lemon juice. Add just enough cold water to barely cover the apples. Put over a low heat and simmer gently until the apples are very soft and pulpy – about 1 hour. Remove the pan from the heat.

2 Mash the apples, then pour the mixture into a scalded jelly bag (available from good cook shops). Leave the mixture to drip through the jelly bag for about 1½ hours, until there are hardly any drips. Do not squeeze the bag.

3 Discard the pulp in the jelly bag. Measure the quantity of strained apples, then pour them into the cleaned pan or preserving pan and bring to the boil. Remove from the heat.

4 For each 2½ cups of measured strained apple, add 2 cups sugar to the pan and stir until dissolved. Return to the heat, bring to the boil and boil rapidly until setting point is reached. The mixture should reach a temperature of 220°F – test with a jelly thermometer. Remove from the heat and leave the mixture to settle for about 15 minutes.

5 Add the chopped mint and stir well to distribute it, then

pour the jelly into warmed,
sterilized jars (see page 4). Seal
and label.

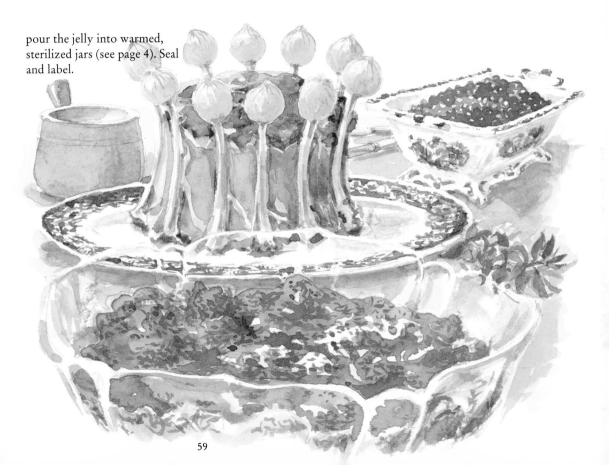

REDCURRANT & ROSEMARY JELLY

The jelly makes an excellent accompaniment to roast pork and cold cooked meats.

1 Put the redcurrants into a large pan or preserving pan with the water and lemon juice. Heat gently and simmer until the fruit is very tender, about 30 minutes.

2 Mash the fruit, then pour it into a scalded jelly bag (available from good cook shops). Leave the mixture to drip through the jelly bag for about 40 minutes, until there are hardly any drips. Do not squeeze the bag.

3 Return the pulp in the jelly bag to the

pan with a further 1¼ cups water and simmer for 30 minutes more, then strain the mixture again. Discard the remaining pulp.

4 Mix together the two quantities of strained juice, and measure the amount. Pour into the cleaned pan or preserving pan and bring to the boil. Remove from the heat. For each 2½ cups of fruit juice, add 2 cups sugar to the pan and stir until dissolved. Return the pan to the heat, bring to the boil, and boil rapidly until

setting point is reached. The mixture should reach a temperature of 220°F – test with a jelly thermometer.

5 Scald the sprigs of rosemary with boiling water and add a couple of sprigs to each warmed, sterilized jar (see page 4). Pour in the redcurrant jelly, then seal and label.

RASPBERRY VINEGAR

Richly colored and juicy raspberries make this superb fruit vinegar, which tastes marvelous in salad dressings.

MAKES 3 PINTS

3 quarts raspberries

5 cups distilled white malt vinegar

3 cups granulated sugar

whole raspberries to decorate (optional)

1 Put the raspberries into a large glass mixing bowl and mash them with a wooden spoon or potato masher. Add the vinegar and stir well. Cover the bowl with plastic wrap and leave to stand in a cool place for 1 week, stirring several times each day.

2 Strain the mixture through a jelly bag (available from good cook shops). When the bag has stopped dripping, squeeze it to extract as much of the fruit vinegar as possible.

3 Measure the amount of liquid and pour it into a large pan. Add 1 cup of sugar to each 2½ cups of liquid. Heat gently, stirring, to dissolve the sugar, then boil rapidly for 10 minutes.

4 Pour into warmed, sterilized bottles (see page 4). Add a few whole raspberries to each bottle if liked, and seal with vinegar-proof tops.

Raspberry Vinegar

INDEX